PICTURE LIBRARY

SNAKES

PICTURE LIBRARY
SNAKES

Norman Barrett

Franklin Watts

London   New York   Sydney   Toronto

© 1989 Franklin Watts Ltd

First published in Great Britain
    1989 by
Franklin Watts Ltd
12a Golden Square
London W1R 4BA

First published in the USA by
Franklin Watts Inc
387 Park Avenue South
New York
NY 10016

First published in Australia by
Franklin Watts
14 Mars Road
Lane Cove
NSW 2066

UK ISBN: 0 86313 812 8
US ISBN: 0-531-10701-9
Library of Congress Catalog Card
Number 88-51513

Printed in Italy

Designed by
Barrett & Weintroub

Photographs by
Survival Anglia
Zoological Society of London
N. S. Barrett

Illustration by
Rhoda & Robert Burns

Technical Consultant
Michael Chinery

Contents

Introduction

Most people regard snakes as objects of fear. But few snakes are harmful to human beings, and some are among the most colorful members of the animal kingdom.

Snakes vary in size, from a few inches long to as much as 10 meters (over 30 ft). They are found mainly in tropical lands, but most countries have some snakes. They live in forests, deserts, rivers and seas. Some live underground.

△ A fearsome sight, the gaping jaws of an African rock python. Pythons are among the largest snakes. They are constrictors, squeezing and suffocating their prey before eating it.

Snakes are reptiles. There are about 2,700 kinds of snakes. They are related to lizards, turtles, alligators and crocodiles.

Some snakes are poisonous. Others, called constrictors, squeeze and suffocate their prey.

A snake's skin is dry and smooth, and covered with scales. Snakes have no legs. They usually move about by wriggling on their belly.

△ An adder, or northern viper. Adders are found all over Europe, even in the cold of the Arctic Circle. They are poisonous snakes.

7

Looking at snakes

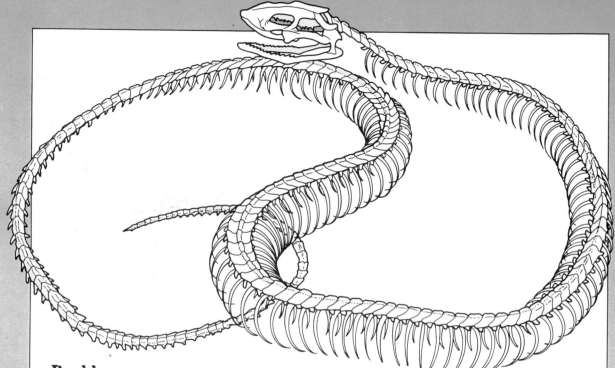

Backbone

Snakes have a large number of bones in their backbone. Some kinds of python have as many as 400. Powerful muscles attached to the bones enable snakes to twist themselves into smooth coils.

Jaws

The jaws of most snakes are so loosely attached to each other and

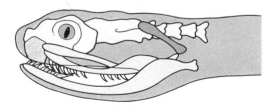

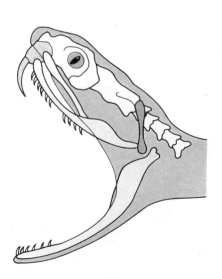

to their skulls that they can open their mouths very wide. This enables them to swallow prey much wider than their own heads.

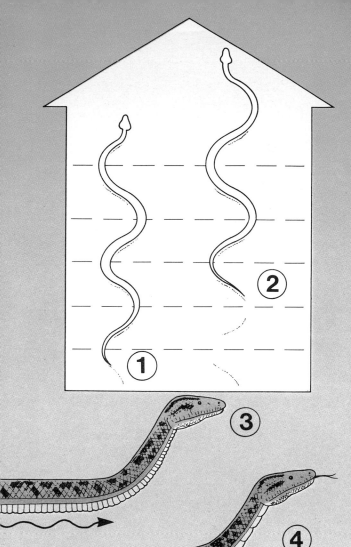

How a snake moves

Most snakes move with a winding, wriggling motion (1 and 2). Using the muscles connecting the skin to the ribs, they push back against stones, vegetation or any roughness of the ground. This pressure has the effect of thrusting their body forward. The whole body follows the direction of the head as it moves along.

The method used by heavy snakes such as pythons and boas is like that of a caterpillar (3 and 4). They use the wide scales that run across their belly to grip the ground and pull them along in a straight line.

Size of snakes

One of the biggest snakes is the South American anaconda, weighing as much as 150 kg (330 lb), more than the heaviest of footballers. Anacondas measure as much as 9 m (30 ft), five times the length of a tall human being, and some kinds of python are even longer.

The life of snakes

Most snakes lay eggs, although some, such as adders and anacondas, have live young. The young are left to fend for themselves at birth.

Snakes are cold-blooded animals – that is, they take on the temperature of their surroundings. In regions with cold climates, snakes hibernate during the winter.

Snakes shed, or slough, their skin several times a year.

▽ A rattlesnake sloughing its skin. The skin splits at the upper lip and the head comes out first. The snake is temporarily blind as the eye covering comes away. Note the tongue flicking out. Snakes do this to pick up scent.

△ A reticulated python with her eggs. Unlike birds' eggs, snakes' eggs have soft shells and the embryo inside is well developed before the egg is laid. Most kinds of snakes lay from 5 to 30 eggs. Large pythons produce 50 eggs or more.

◁ An anaconda with her live young just after birth. Some kinds of snakes bear more than a hundred baby snakes at one time.

11

Spot the snake

Snakes have long, thin bodies and most of them move slowly, so they need to keep well hidden from their enemies and from their own prey. Most snakes blend in with their surroundings. This is called natural camouflage.

The snakes on these pages are not easy to spot at first glance: adders (left), a python in a rocky water hole (below), a twig snake (right), Cliffords snake (opposite, below right) and a tree snake (opposite, below left).

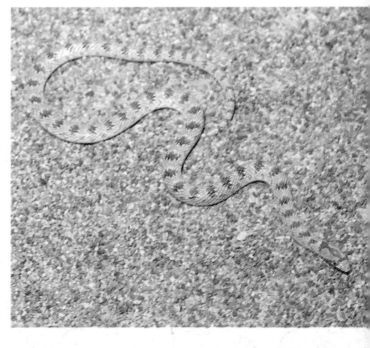

Vipers

Vipers are poisonous snakes with long fangs at the front of their mouths. The fangs are hinged, and can be folded away when not in use. Vipers bite their victims with their fangs and inject them with venom (poison).

There are two main kinds of vipers, pit vipers and true vipers. Pit vipers have pit organs between their eyes and nostrils which enable them to locate their prey by its body heat.

▽ The rhinoceros viper, or nose-horned viper, is so called because of the pair of scales that stick out just above the nostrils. It is a true viper and is found in the tropical forests of Africa.

△ The eyelash viper of
Central America is a
brightly colored pit
viper.

◁ Another pit viper, the
western diamondback
rattlesnake, is one of the
most dangerous of the
North American snakes.

The rattle of a rattlesnake is at the end of its tail. Rapid movement of the tail causes it to vibrate and make the familiar rattling sound.

The purpose of the rattle is not known for certain, but it may be to draw the attention of enemies or prey to the snake's tail rather than its head. The rattle consists of a series of horny, shell-like rings. A new ring is added every time the snake sloughs its skin.

△ The prairie rattlesnake of the United States is a species of diamondback with irregular markings. The pits below the eyes are clearly visible, as are the rings on its rattle.

▷ The sidewinder is a small American rattlesnake, so-called because, like some other desert-living snakes, it moves over the sand with a sideways motion.

▷ The American copper-head is a beautifully marked pit viper. Most copper-heads are small, about 80 cm (2½ ft) long, and because they are also silent they are not as readily noticed as rattlesnakes and cause more bites. Their bite is seldom fatal to adults, but is dangerous to children.

The cobra family

Cobras are highly poisonous snakes that live mainly in Africa and southern Asia. Some cobras bite their victims with fixed front fangs. Other kinds squirt, or spit, poison through the air at their victims' eyes.

Cobras belong to the elapid family. Other elapids include the mambas of Africa, the coral snakes of the Americas and the taipans and tiger snakes of Australia.

△ A black spitting cobra from Africa in defensive pose. When cobras are nervous or enraged, they flatten and spread their neck into a "hood."

▷ The king cobra of south eastern Asia preys on other snakes. It is the longest poisonous snake, measuring as much as 5 m (16 ft).

▽ A coral snake in Arizona. Coral snakes have colorful bands and are western relatives of the cobra. They range from the southern United States to tropical South America. They have a poisonous bite and are also snake-eaters.

Constrictors

Constrictors are snakes that coil around their prey and suffocate it before swallowing it.

The largest snakes, pythons, boas and anacondas, are all constrictors and belong to the boid family. Most boids live in hot lands. Different kinds live in trees, on the ground or in water.

King snakes also suffocate their prey. They are harmless to humans but eat other snakes and small animals.

▽ An African python swallows a squirrel. Constrictors do not crush the bones or change the shape of their victims. They wind themselves around their prey and tighten their coils to stop it breathing. They then swallow the prey head first. Large animals can take several days to digest.

△ A boa constrictor of Costa Rica. Boa constrictors live in tropical parts of the Americas. They are from 3 to 4 m (10–13 ft) long. They usually hunt from trees, attacking animals as they pass beneath them.

◁ The anaconda is found in tropical South America. Anacondas live in or near water and are also called water boas.

△ The rainbow boa of South America usually rests in trees during the day and hunts at night.

◁ The emerald tree boa lives in the tropical rain forests of South America.

▷ An Arizona Mountain king snake climbs a tree in the Sonoran Desert. Although similar in color to coral snakes, king snakes are not related to them and are not poisonous.

▽ A California king snake swallows a whiptail lizard. King snakes also eat other snakes, even rattlesnakes, and are immune to (safe from) their poison.

Other kinds of snakes

◁ A boomslang, a back-fanged snake from Africa, crawls into the nest of a weaverbird in search of prey. Although most back-fanged snakes are usually harmless to people because they need to chew their prey in order to inject venom, the boomslang has been known to kill human beings.

▽ An egg-eating snake of Africa has one meal inside it and another waiting to be eaten. Spikes inside the snake's throat crack the shell, which is then cast out.

The harmless European grass snake (top left); a tiny West African burrowing snake (middle left), which measures about 10 cm (4 in); the long-nosed tree snake of South East Asia (bottom left), which has a flat body and, unlike most other snakes, horizontal pupils; a harmless tree snake from Mexico (top); a long-nosed snake from Arizona (above); and a golden-banded mangrove snake from Indonesia (below).

△ A flying snake from Indonesia. Flying snakes sometimes launch themselves from a high branch and glide to the ground. They do this by pulling their belly in to produce a sort of parachute effect.

◁ An eastern hog-nosed snake of the United States. Hog-nosed snakes flatten their neck when threatened, or even turn over and pretend to be dead.

▷ The smooth snake is found in parts of northern Europe, including southern England.

▷ A brown water snake swallows a catfish in the marshy Everglades of Florida.

▽ An eastern ribbon snake, a kind of garter snake. Garter snakes are small, harmless snakes that live in North and Central America and are often found in city parks and back yards.

The story of snakes

The reptiles

Snakes belong to the reptile branch of the animal kingdom. Their closest relatives are lizards. Most scientists believe that snakes developed from lizards millions of years ago. Snakes and lizards make up about 95 percent of all the different kinds of reptiles alive today. Reptiles that have become extinct (no longer living) include the dinosaurs.

The Garden of Eden

In the Biblical story of Adam and Eve, the serpent in the Garden of Eden that tempted Eve with forbidden fruit was a snake. The serpent represented the devil. But snakes have not always been associated with evil. In many places, snakes have been worshiped as gods.

Snakes in mythology

The ancient Egyptians worshiped snakes as symbols of fertility, associating them with the River Nile. The ancient Greeks regarded the snake as a symbol of healing, because of its ability to shed its old skin and reappear healthier and stronger.

But snakes and serpents are often the "bad guys" in ancient mythology, the traditional stories

△ A group of statues carved over 2,000 years ago shows the Trojan priest Laocoön and his sons being crushed by sea serpents.

of gods and heroes. In ancient Greece, a mythical monster called Python is said to have attacked people and cattle. The god Apollo killed it with arrows when he was five days old.

Another Greek legend tells of the priest Laocoön, who warned the Trojans not to accept the wooden horse left outside their walls by the besieging Greeks.

△ Snake charmers in India.

But Laocoön and his sons were crushed to death by serpents that came out of the sea. The Trojans then took the wooden horse in, and during the night Greek soldiers came out of the horse and captured the city.

Fascination of snakes

It seems that there is something about snakes that fascinates people, even if they are afraid of them. The larger snakes especially are prized exhibits in zoos. In North Africa and India, snake charmers have mystified and entertained audiences for many years. Some people keep snakes as pets, but snakes cannot show affection.

△ Early days in the Bronx Zoo, New York, and the keepers are struggling with their new exhibit, a large python.

Survival

The biggest danger to the survival of snakes in the wild is

△ The manager of a wildlife refuge in Florida with a protected indigo snake.

the destruction of their natural habitats. There is also a trade in snake skin for such items as bags and shoes, and in a few places people eat snake meat. Some species (kinds) of snakes are protected by law.

In some parts of the United States, "rattlesnake round-ups" are organized. In these, hundreds of snakes are collected, often driven from their homes, and mistreated and killed for amusement.

△ Men pump gas into a rattlesnake den during a "rattlesnake round-up."

Facts and records

Abnormalities

As with most animals, abnormally colored snakes are not uncommon. Other freaks of nature also occur. Even two-headed snakes are sometimes found.

△ Implanting a small radio transmitter in a snake so that its movements can be monitored.

they always go back to the same places.

Producing an antidote

Poisonous snakes may be "milked" of their venom. The venom is collected and made into an antidote, a cure for the snake's bite.

△ A two-headed gopher snake of the American prairies.

Spring journey

Scientists studying the habits of prairie rattlers in Wyoming have made an interesting discovery. The snakes collect in caves to hibernate during the winter. In spring, after mating, the males leave the caves, where there is enough food only for the females and young, and travel as much as 50 km (30 miles). They later return, and experiments with radio implants have shown that

△ A snake's fangs are forced over the edge of a funnel so that its venom may be "milked."

Glossary

Antidote
A medicine that stops the effects of a poison.

Boids (pronounced bo-ids)
A family of large snakes including pythons, boas and anacondas.

Camouflage
Coloring and shape of an animal that helps it hide from its enemies and prey by blending in with its surroundings.

Constrictors
Snakes that coil around their prey and suffocate it.

Elapids
A family of poisonous snakes that includes cobras, mambas, coral snakes, taipans, tiger snakes and some very poisonous sea snakes.

Embryo
A young animal in its early stages of development, before birth.

Extinct
No longer existing.

Fangs
Teeth through which snakes inject venom into their prey.

Garter snakes
A group of harmless snakes, most of which have three light stripes running the length of the body.

Natural habitat
The normal place in the wild where a particular animal lives.

Pits
Organs that enable certain snakes to detect their prey by its body heat.

Reptiles
A branch of the animal kingdom that includes snakes, lizards, alligators, crocodiles and turtles.

Slough
To shed (the skin).

Venom
A snake's poison, which it injects into its victims by biting. As a means of defense, some kinds of cobra discharge their venom by spitting it.

Vipers
A family of snakes that have long, hinged fangs at the front of their mouth. Vipers include adders and rattlesnakes.

Index